On Mao Tse-tung's Book of Quotations

by Nicholas Jay Boyes

www.ecologicalera.com

contactnicholas@ecologicalera.com

ISBN 978-0-557-38283-5

Table of Contents

Introduction

I wrote this manuscript in 2009 approximately a year or two after receiving this book from a friend who personally visited China. It was interesting to read and critique something so current, generally I find myself in the books of Karl Marx and Friedrich Engels, well into the realm of the 19th century.

China has a long history, and it would be wrong to simply see Mao Tse Tung as not representative of China's long history. Mao plays a modern role in China as a leader of the people, a Marxist Leninist with revolutionary experience in the communist revolution.

In my first approach to this book I must admit I felt apprehension towards Mao. I thought China was too far away from America to really grasp anything Mao wrote, that the Chinese revolution might be too far away to really be able to embrace any of its philosophy. After all, it is the other side of the Earth.

I'm happy to say I found the book to be quite good, and it has had an influence on me. Mao's thoughts are widely misunderstood in the West. Although there are many passages of the book I found not worth commenting on, largely due to the fact I was looking for political economy and philosophical ideas, rather than martial arts or party organization thoughts, the overall content of Mao's book seems to be an attempt to validate the ideas of Marx, Engels, and Lenin.

There is an old saying in America that goes something like: If you can't say something good about something, don't say anything at all…

In this respect I found objectionable thoughts by Mao, conquering nature, for instance. Nevertheless I also found a great depth and feeling of someone who legitimately was trying to do the right thing as China's leader. His wisdom, for instance defeat strengthens us, as we see the hand of the enemy, is invaluable today.

As a new millennium thinker I tried to find the relevant passages in the book to my bent, political economy and philosophy. Thus I skipped over some of the material.

One could say I should have been more critical of some of the ideas that were contradictory, or off the subject. In all respect I could have been more critical, but I think writing about the good in a book and skipping over the bad is a statement in itself. It shows what is right, by paying attention to the right thoughts, and leaves open the possibility of discussion.

Undoubtedly there are some who approach this type of writing and look only for the mistakes and outdated ideas. This to me seems like an unwise move, it is too rigid, and does not allow for the inevitable errors made by the human being.

Mao was a human being, and human beings do the best they can under the circumstances they find themselves in. As a leader of the people Mao gave it his best shot, and this book shows he was a wise man….

I would like to thank friends who got me the book from China, Alexander Boyes my brother who helped me edit this work, and family who gave me the inspiration to write this book, and lastly the Marxist Internet Archive. Many Thanks.

Nicholas Jay Boyes

8 15 2009

Chapter 1

On China's Historical Position in Society

"The force at the core leading our cause forward is the Chinese Communist Party. The theoretical basis guiding our thinking is Marxism-Leninism.

-Opening address at the First Session of the First National People's Congress of the People's Republic of China (September 15, 1954).

http://www.marxists.org/reference/archive/mao/works/red-book/ch02.htm

All passages here fore shall be quoted from this location.

The theoretical basis of Chinese thought is definitely Marxist Leninist. Although there were breaks in the past between the two parties, Soviet Bolsheviks and Chinese communists, in particular in the 80's, China has remained loyal to the Marxist Leninist cause.

It is of historical significance to note in the 80's Soviet society was failing, and the constant concessions to capitalism were beginning. It reaches a crescendo into the early 90's until Soviet society completely fails.

China in this respect saw clearly the direction Soviet society was travelling, and the conflict between the two of the powers in the countries, respectively, begins historically to make more sense. Perhaps

China saw the immanent failure of the Soviets to follow Marxist Leninist thought, and went their own direction.

Regardless of the past, China remains Marxist Leninist, although of late capitalism has been slowly returning. But one must remember China is a large country with many people, and change takes time. Nevertheless they remain Marxist Leninist, and are a powerful nation…

" If there is to be revolution, there must be a revolutionary party. Without a revolutionary party, without a party built on the Marxist-Leninist revolutionary theory and in the Marxist-Leninist revolutionary style, it is impossible to lead the working class and the broad masses of the people in defeating imperialism and its running dogs.

-"Revolutionary Forces of the World Unite, Fight Against Imperialist Aggression!" (November 1948), Selected Works, Vol. IV, p. 284.*

The idea of a leaderless revolution is like a ship with no captain. Need we suggest it is destined to crash on the rocks, especially if the deckhands bicker over where to steer next?

Obviously leadership is needed to form a successful revolution. Anarchy, romantic revolutionary notions, are abstractions. A hierarchical structure is a necessity for a party to exist, with the ability for orders to come from ideas below and be acted upon by the top.

Those who do take power must realize it is not something to be desired, rather a social obligation forced on the person by the community. Those who do desire power must be closely watched by those who profess to follow. Otherwise we get leadership that is class, with material rewards for membership, and the endless jobs of bureaucrat and dignitary, a middle class....

"No political party can possibly lead a great revolutionary movement to victory unless it possesses revolutionary theory and knowledge of history and has a profound grasp of the practical movement.

-"The Role of the Chinese Communist Party in the National War" (October 1938), Selected Works, Vol. II, p. 208.

Recognition of the historical position of the proletariat, as regards the national conditions of a culture, is of paramount importance. Revolutionary knowledge must be the light guiding the movement forward, in particular Marxism.

History creates the conditions one finds himself in, but he is not powerless to change history. Men create their own history, and when men begin to realize a better future is possible they begin to attempt to control history. This is emancipation.

Chapter 2

Changes in Society

"Classes struggle, some classes triumph, others are eliminated. Such is history; such is the history of civilization for thousands of years. To interpret history from this viewpoint is historical materialism; standing in opposition to this viewpoint is historical idealism.

-"Cast Away Illusions, Prepare for Struggle" (August 14, 1949), Selected Works, Vol. IV, p. 428.

Quotations from Mao Tse Tung
Little Red Book of Quotations
Marxists Internet Archive
http://www.marxists.org/reference/archive/mao/works/red-book/

It is of interest to the Western socialists in particular to see that the old Asiatic societies recognized they had class distinctions that were counter productive to attaining a higher degree of culture. Mao saw the class structure in China, a society differing from the west in its ancient history, a culture that existed well before America, and even most of Europe and aggressively challenged it.

Historical materialism is recognizing the material causes of the economic and political changes in society, it is historical because it places a given level of cultural development as a historical phenomenon, not an eternal relationship. Historical materialism sees the transient nature of social needs, that some things, i.e. cars, are part of a historical movement of the political and economic structure of society, and are intimately connected to the natural sciences, which with the engineers and scientist allow for a certain pattern of thought to be created, based on scientific reasoning i.e. Galileo's telescope and the Earth revolving around the sun.

"Changes in society are due chiefly to the development of the internal contradictions in society, that is, the contradiction between the productive forces and the relations of production, the contradiction between classes and the contradiction between the old and the new; it is the development of these contradictions that pushes society forward and gives the impetus for the suppression of the old society by the new.

-"On Contradiction" (August 1937), Selected Works, Vol. I, P. 314. Mao ibid. (see above)

Development of the productive forces of industry creates a proletariat, as the industrial capitalist replaces manufacture with the modern capitalist factory. The large numbers of workers who do not own the means of production creates a class of men, the proletariat, whose purpose is to labor for the lowest possible wage, that of the universal social value, minimum wage. Capital, by its essence moveable property, always maintains the lowest wage possible for simple survival of the worker, and its transient nature, never staying long in one location, another one of its amazing abilities to create surplus value, and keep down wages.

The change of society to the modern industrial capitalist in control of industry was an upheaval felt by all of Europe, i.e. French revolution. At first it was good for the peasant, as the large landed estates were broken, replaced by small holdings. Even Napoleon Bonaparte when viewed this way was not so bad.

Unfortunately for the peasants it did not last long, as industry revolutionized the relationship of man to the land, and eventually gave way to the modern industrial farming we now know, using the tractor. This movement totally replaced the peasant with the proletariat, as people moved into the cities to get jobs in the factory. In America by the turn of the millennium about 5% of its people were farming, and 85% a proletariat, the remaining 10% the bourgeoisie and it sympathizers, the middle class.

"The ruthless economic exploitation and political oppression of the peasants by the landlord class forced them into numerous uprisings against its rule.... It was the class struggles of the peasants, the peasant uprisings and peasant wars that constituted the real motive force of historical development in Chinese feudal society.

-"The Chinese Revolution and the Chinese Communist Party" (December 1939), Selected Works, Vol. II, p. 308.*

Mao ibid. (see above)

The old Asiatic society, under the almost caste conditions, was found in modern Tibet. Lacking railroads, radios, television, the people were divided into peasants and a feudal upper class. The monks, who had a numerically large size compared to the feudal ruling class, did not work. The Dali Lama was considered to be a living god and the monks his following. The laborer on the land after the revolution saw his wages double as the monks were no longer supported by him as much as prior.

In more industrialized countries the struggle of the classes occurs in the factory and large city, as under these conditions the proletariat flourishes.

This in no way places the labourers of the less industrialized country as less than equals, rather places the less developed worlds movement more in the country rather than in the city. Peasant is not an undignified thing to be called...

"A revolution is not a dinner party, or writing an essay, or painting a picture, or doing embroidery; it cannot be so refined, so leisurely and gentle, so temperate, kind, courteous, restrained and magnanimous. A revolution is an insurrection, an act of violence by which one class overthrows another.

"Report on an Investigation of the Peasant Movement in Hunan" (March 1927), Selected Works, Vol. I, p. 28.*

A revolution can definitely take the shape and form of a guerrilla struggle. We have seen this repeatedly, everywhere from Central America to Southeast Asia. The revolution responds to the violence perpetrated by the bourgeoisie against the labourer with an equal amount of retaliation.

Bloodshed almost seems inevitable, as the bourgeoisie clings to power against the new force unleashed by their own society.

In all due respect China has had a martial arts history dating back before recorded history. It should not shock us they see violence as an effective way of replacing private property with socialism. Once the universal suffrage of capitalists is no longer present the society edges toward revolution, and rooting out he reactionaries responsible becomes the purpose of dictatorship…

"I hold that it is bad as far as we are concerned if a person, a political party, an army or a school is not attacked by the enemy, for in that case it would definitely mean that we have sunk to the level of the enemy. It is good if we are attacked by the enemy, since it proves that we have drawn a clear line of demarcation between the enemy and ourselves. It is still better if the enemy attacks us wildly and paints us as utterly black and without a single virtue; it demonstrates that we have not only drawn a clear line of demarcation between the enemy and ourselves but achieved a great deal in our work.

-To Be Attacked by the Enemy Is Not a Bad Thing but a Good Thing (May 26, 1939), first pocket ed., p. two. *

This revolutionary theory of Mao holds true today, that to be attacked by the enemy should be expected. The historical position of the proletariat in the American Democratic Republic corresponds to a culture similar to martial law, remember the most barbaric of attacks instigated by the supposedly less reactionary Democratic Party under Bill Clinton and Albert Gore, contender for the capitalist rubber stamp of the Nobel Peace Prize and continued by the Republican Party of George Bush bourgeoisie throughout the new millennium. The daily struggle of the proletariat to live, blacklisted, hated by the bourgeois and branded a common criminal, wounded by civil strife but still persevering, are the real tale of the class struggle, of the brutal shock of body on body between the bourgeoisie and it workers.

Being attacked constantly for ones political beliefs is a mark of a civil struggle. The act of the aggressor to attack the labourer clearly demarcates the boundary between the classes.

Defeat teaches one patience, a virtue connected with good things coming to those who wait.

The proletariat has been very patient. It is one of their strongest attributes, connected with the ability to take the blow on the chin.

The most important lesson for the labourer is to see and know the real assessment of his condition by the bourgeois. Only then will Communist Party be able to grow, the realization of the labourer he is oppressed, and that the other labourers are no longer afraid of secrecy and have cast aside their differences and taken the rebellious step of being willing to be called this, Communist Party.

"In China, although in the main socialist transformation has been completed with respect to the system of ownership, and although the large-scale and turbulent class struggles of the masses characteristic of the previous revolutionary periods have in the main come to an end, there are still remnants of the overthrown landlord and comprador classes, there is still a bourgeoisie, and the remolding of the petty bourgeoisie has only just started. The class struggle is by no means over. The class struggle between the proletariat and the bourgeoisie, the class struggle between the different political forces, and the class struggle in the ideological held between the proletariat and the bourgeoisie will continue to be long and tortuous and at times will even become very acute. The proletariat seeks to transform the world according to its own world outlook, and so does the bourgeoisie. In this respect, the question of which will win out, socialism or capitalism, is still not really settled.

-On the Correct Handling of Contradictions among the People (February 27, 1957), 1st pocket ed., pp. 51-52.

Mao Tse Tung ibid. (see above)

It is sad to say that although this was written by Mao in 1957, today the same problems plague Chinese society. The insidious bourgeois finds his way into all structures, and the growth of an above ground bourgeoisie in China threatens all Mao Tse Tung and the revolution stood for. Creation of a national lottery, to place a new oppressor in a position to command working class labour, later inevitably through stock ownership, a stock market in place, etc. are all symptoms of the fall of the communists in China. Indeed, the class struggle in China is by no means won, and unfortunately it is increasingly looking like the bourgeoisie will triumph, as the weak kneed party bureaucratic structure is easily corrupted by material incentives, cell phones, cars, etc. all the excesses of the bourgeois in America. A real revolution will require recognizing the true nature of all wealth, created by labour, and wasted labour the oppression of the proletariat.

"It will take a long period to decide the issue in the ideological struggle between socialism and capitalism in our country. The reason is that the influence of the bourgeoisie and of the intellectuals who come from the old society will remain in our country for a long time to come, and so will their class ideology. If this is not sufficiently understood, or is not understood at all, the gravest mistakes will be made and the necessity of waging the struggle in the ideological field will be ignored.

-Ibid. pp. 52-53.
On the Correct Handling of Contradictions among the People (February 27, 1957), 1st pocket ed., pp. 51-52.

Indeed the class struggle of China's proletariat has taken a long time, and is by no means settled, even after a violent revolution placing the Communist Party of China in charge of the state. Vague far off promises of more equality with bourgeois democracy, of a level playing field so one man can have more than another, as well as feudal religious belief, misunderstanding the relationship between the creation of wealth and alienation of the labourer towards its product, all remain as problems which must be addressed by the labourers if removal of the bourgeois is still the goal.

"In our country bourgeois and petty-bourgeois ideology, anti-Marxist ideology will continue to exist for a long time. Basically, the socialist system has been established in our country. We have won the basic victory in transforming the ownership of the means of production, but we have not yet won complete victory on the political and ideological fronts. In the ideological field, the question of who will win in the struggle between the proletariat and the bourgeoisie has not been really settled yet. We still have to wage a protracted struggle against bourgeois and petty bourgeois ideology. It is wrong not to understand this and to give up ideological struggle. All erroneous ideas, all poisonous weeds, all ghosts and monsters, must be subjected to criticism; in no circumstance should they be allowed to spread unchecked. However, the criticism should be fully reasoned, analytical and convincing, and not rough, bureaucratic, metaphysical or dogmatic.

-Speech at the Chinese Communist Party's National Conference on Propaganda Work (March 12, 1957), 1st pocket ed., and pp. 26-27.

The hard work of creating a society that accepts socialism was completed in China, but still the old society of capitalism continues to rear its head, in the form of bond ownership by the state. Currently the Chinese own 1.7 trillion dollars in interest bearing national bonds in the United States. These investments keep the bourgeoisie in America afloat, guaranteeing the ability of the American capitalist to create surplus value.

The first problem with the bond ownership is it transforms China's state into a capitalist, attempting to attain surplus value from the labourer, in this case in America. Just as taxation can be offensive, even though the bourgeois hold the purse strings in Congress for nationalized industry, paying the state for labour to help the Chinese state is really no different than paying the American state.

By creating the state as a capitalist China effectively taxes the American worker. The tax is felt when the money bears interest...

Were the bonds owned out of the kindness of the proletariat of China they would place restrictions on what the money is used for. With 70 cents out of every tax dollar going to the military, where the Chinese bonds are going should be clear. And the military spending in America under Obama continues to grow...

China could help the proletariat by immediately cashing in all bonds, and asking for hard currency for the bonds. If the state bankrupted capitalism would fail...

Chapter 3

Socialism and Communism

"Communism is at once a complete system of proletarian ideology and a new social system. It is different from any other ideological and social system, and is the most complete, progressive, revolutionary and rational system in human history. The ideological and social system of feudalism has a place only in the museum of history. The ideological and social system of capitalism has also become a museum piece in one part of the world (in the Soviet Union), while in other countries it resembles "a dying person who is sinking fast, like the sun setting beyond the western hills", and will soon be relegated to the museum. The communist ideological and social system alone is full of youth and vitality, sweeping the world with the momentum of an avalanche and the force of a thunderbolt.

-"On New Democracy" (January 1940), Selected Works, Vol. II, pp. 360-61. *

Communism, the lack of surplus value in production, differs from all preceding systems of government. It is not feudalism, as it removes all hereditary titles to power. It is no longer capitalism as there is no a bourgeoisie in power creating surplus value. It is a working system of the labourers in control of production, the producers of commodities in control of their own labour, making the decisions of what and how commodities will be produced.

It is a radical shift from inheritance and hereditary titles to ownership of the means of production. Prior to recent history it was never tried. Karl Marx's discovery of surplus value made socialism as a scientific system, dialectical materialism, possible.

It is a product of the industrial revolution, and is connected with the steam engine and locomotive, rather than Adam Smith who only had the horse and carriage to work with. It is a product of the latest philosophers in Europe, in the 19th century especially, and then later in the 20th, applied after a revolution as a world power, the Soviet Union. It is not the "old government", "old system" etc. It is a truly novel idea created by the latest European philosophers and political economists.

"The socialist system will eventually replace the capitalist system; this is an objective law independent of man's will. However much the reactionaries try to hold back the wheel of history, eventually revolution will take place and will inevitably triumph.

-Speech at the Meeting of the Supreme Soviet of the USSR in Celebration of the 40th Anniversary of the Great October Socialist Revolution" (November 6, 1957)

The socialist revolution may triumph, but Mao is mistaken of its inevitability. Socialism does not naturally occur without a push from the proletariat, it requires actions.

Socialism will not occur and society will slide backwards without the constant everyday pressure from the proletariat to create it. Mao himself said the revolution requires action, and even risking ones life for the cause.

The Chinese proletariat have overthrown capitalism. They must not now rest but continue to struggle to emancipate labour from its previous conditions of production for surplus value. If they do not they will shortly follow the fate of the Soviet Union, and be overthrown by the bourgeoisie...

"We Communists never conceal our political views. Definitely and beyond all doubt, our future or maximum program is to carry China forward to socialism and communism. Both the name of our Party and our Marxist world outlook unequivocally point to this supreme ideal of the future, a future of incomparable brightness and splendor.

-"On Coalition Government" (April 24, 1945), Selected Works, Vol. III, p. 282. *

Obviously it is no secret to the bourgeoisie who is who in society. The communists are a product of the class struggle, a nominal term to describe those who are not fitting into the class structure, who reject the division of labour...

Communism is striven for by communists due to the revolution to remove the act of creation of surplus value.

Secrecy regarding membership into this hated category of the bourgeois is only due to fear of retaliation. The fear is of necessity to the owners of private property, fear of the communists.

Why one who realized he was being called this would deny to the fellow labourer his status is only ignorance.

The grouping of the Jewish people in western society into the communist category, as Western Europe did in the 20th century; Germany in particular, is no obstacle. The communist movement is atheist, but the Jewish people are a good honorable race of men, and discrimination against the Jew should offend those who want equality. Thus there is no real obstacle to being grouped as a Jew, it is simply nominally a common mistake nothing one should be offended by....

"Taken as a whole, the Chinese revolutionary movement led by the Communist Party embraces the two stages, i.e., the democratic and the socialist revolutions, which are two essentially different revolutionary processes, and the second process can be carried through only after the first has been completed. The democratic revolution is the necessary preparation for the socialist revolution, and the socialist revolution is the inevitable sequel to the democratic revolution. The ultimate aim for which all communists strive is to bring about a socialist and communist society.

-"The Chinese Revolution and the Chinese Communist Party" (December 1939), Selected Works, Vol. II, pp. 330-31. *

The constant saber rattling of the forces of the American bourgeoisie towards what they say is oppression, namely the dictatorship of the proletariat, must be kept in perspective.

To begin with, women were only grated the right to vote after agitations finally resulting in women's universal suffrage in 1921. This was about 5 years after the Russian revolution. Black people were denied Universal Suffrage until 1965 in America.

"The National Voting Rights Act of 1965 (42 U.S.C. § 1973–1973aa-6)[1] outlawed discriminatory voting practices that had been responsible for the widespread disenfranchisement (definition: legally unable to vote ed.) of African Americans in the United States. Echoing the language of the 15th Amendment, the Act prohibited states from imposing any "voting qualification or prerequisite to voting, or standard, practice, or procedure ... to deny or abridge the right of any citizen of the United States to vote on account of race or color."[2] Specifically, Congress intended the Act to outlaw the practice of requiring otherwise qualified voters to pass literacy tests in order to register to vote, a principal means by which Southern states had prevented African-Americans from exercising the franchise.[3] The Act was signed into law by President Lyndon B. Johnson, a Democrat, who had earlier signed the landmark Civil Rights Act of 1964 into law.

-Wikipedia 2009

As we can see it was only in 1964 the Americans allowed all their citizens to vote. This was 16 years after Mao and his communists took power in China.

This must be remembered when dealing with democratic revolutions, they proceed from dictatorial conditions.

Universal suffrage is a form of equality, it allows for equal rights of each citizen regardless of class to vote for who he chooses. This is a form of equality like equal rights for all.

Unfortunately this form is is also easily manipulated, and maintained by violence against the proletariat in America. However disguised their intentions may seem, the lack of a socialist party distinguishes the American Democratic Republic of the new millennium...

"Socialist revolution aims at liberating the productive forces. The changeover from individual to socialist, collective ownership in agriculture and handicrafts and from capitalist to socialist ownership in private industry and commerce is bound to bring about a tremendous liberation of the productive forces. Thus, the social conditions are being created for a tremendous expansion of industrial and agricultural production.

-Speech at the Supreme State Conference (January 25, 1956)

The liberation of the productive forces away from private property is what differentiates the socialist revolution from all others in history. Previous revolutions simply replaced one class by another, the communist revolution attempts to remove class altogether. In this respect the democratic revolutions that replace feudalism can be seen as advancement, as the class system was weakened, but it must be said though they are only a changing dynamic that can possibly lead to a socialist revolution, although only through the constant attempts of the exploited class to free itself through political activity. The division of labour led by the Queen to a division of labour dominated by private property being the change of one class for another, effective for a short period, although as history progressed beyond class, outdated…

28

Unfortunately the class system of capitalism brutally reminds us private property can also be very oppressive. The presence of an exploited proletariat, who works hard every day to not even be able to afford health care if he is sick the real reality of the Democratic Republic.

Expansion of production in China occurred well into the new millennium, as China modernized quickly. The first satellites into space were launched in the 20th century, a marker of the development of the productive forces...

In all fairness though it should be noted they were still anthropocentric, and the population doubled even under the Communist Party of China. India also had a population explosion, although with the notable exception of the independence leader Mahatma Gandhi, were not socialist. Of late they were a familial organization, the antithesis of communism. This shows capitalists of the region also had population problems, and one can only imagine China would also have experienced a massive population growth under the capitalists too.

The efforts of China's one child programme were very successful in the cities in the 21st century, and began to tame the explosion in population.

The industrial pollution and the desertification in the north continued to dog the Communist Party into the 21st century.

The ecological movement was a product of the late stages of capitalism and the birth of socialism. Viewed with suspicion by all parties, capitalist and socialist in the 20th century, the movement began to shape culture regardless of the anthropocentric ideas of the early socialists and late capitalists.

Logically China would seem the best off to undergo serous ecological development, through the use of state workers who require no large monetary reasons to do what has to be done, ecological restoration for the sake of the environment and the labourers. Given the proletariat has no country, and no longer sees the territorial boundaries of societies for anything other than a mechanism to divide the workers, China could be in a position to help the Koreas, and Vietnam, at some point.

"...China will energetically increase forest carbon sink and endeavor to increase forest coverage by 40 million hectares and forest stock volume by 1.3 billion cubic meters by 2020 from the 2005 levels, Hu (Jintao) said.

-Xinhua 9 22 2009

The United Nations meeting, which took place in September of 09 showed the clear leadership of China in the struggle for the ecology. Even in a period of economic crisis the leadership of China made a decision to drastically alter the ecology, in a favorable way...

Naturalism and historical materialism are compatible as they both see natural reasons for the development of nature and human society, the latter being a product of natural evolution, a part of the ecology rather than superior or otherwise disconnected from it. Naturalism points to adaptation and evolution as the guide to the progress of the development of a species. Abstractions of creation and an anthropocentric vision of human superiority over the ecology have no place with naturalism. Thus we see materialism, which paces man in control of his development, his ideas the product of historical development, as similar in ideology to naturalism.

Chapter 4

On Agriculture and Production

"We are now carrying out a revolution not only in the social system, the change from private to public ownership, but also in technology, the change from handicraft to large-scale modern machine production, and the two revolutions are interconnected. In agriculture, with conditions as they are in our country co-operation must precede the use of big machinery (in capitalist countries agriculture develops in a capitalist way). Therefore we must on no account regard industry and agriculture, socialist industrialization and the socialist transformation of agriculture as two separate and isolated things, and on no account must we emphasize the one and play down the other.

-On the Question of Agricultural Co-operation (July 51, 1955), 3rd ed., pp. 19-20.

The difference between city and countryside still plagues China, and increasing inequality is but a symptom of a greater failure. Setting the peasant and proletariat to massive ecological construction, i.e. terracing, is only just beginning. Conversely, the American capitalists are even farther away from it, especially in the latest bourgeois adventures in Iraq, where an ecological plan has yet to be advanced as it was never constructed.

Until a massive work programme connecting the proletariat to the countryside in China concretely, as a labour project, the disconnection of town and country will only create worsening conditions of ignorance and inequality, as the people set to work against each other for material gain.

The revolution brought forth by the tractor must emancipate the animal, and the peasant the vehicle for this. It must be the duty of all people in rural and suburban regions to care for livestock and gardens, and for the factory farming of life common in America to be avoided as slavery of the ecology. Growing animals for personal use should be encouraged, and should not be a barrier to collectivization under mechanical agriculture.

"The new social system has only just been established and requires time for its consolidation. It must not be assumed that the new system can be completely consolidated the moment it is established, for that is impossible. It has to be consolidated systematically. To achieve its ultimate consolidation, it is necessary not only to bring about the socialist industrialization of the country and persevere in the socialist revolution on the economic front, but also to carry on constant and arduous socialist revolutionary struggles and socialist education on the political and ideological fronts. Moreover, various contributory international factors are required.

-Speech at the Chinese Communist Party's National Conference on Propaganda Work (March 12, 1957), first pocket ed., and p. two. *

China's opening has been of great importance to the revolution not just in China but in the whole world. Chinese cooking and health are just one of the benefits of China's embracing of international conditions, and have greatly helped the proletariat in the West.

China's social system is modern, yet even through 50 years of revolution is nowhere near completion. Ecological revolution of the countryside must occur; the division of town and country weakened through socialism accomplished.

The tragedy of having to move from the country to the city due to the tractor must be lightened though ability of garden in the city, and have ones own home. This aspect of rapid industrialization, the loss of the relationship of man to ecology, must end. Recognition of man as a dynamic part of a larger community including ecology must occur. In this respect the revolution in China is just beginning…

"In China the struggle to consolidate the socialist system, the struggle to decide whether socialism or capitalism will prevail, will still take a long historical period. However, we should all realize that the new system of socialism will unquestionably be consolidated. We can assuredly build a socialist state with modern industry, modern agriculture, and modern science and culture.

-Ibid. pp. 2-3.

The question of communism is still not yet solved, even with the fall of the Soviet Union. The socialist idea is still fresh in history, the prospect of revolutionary change in the structure of society influenced by a change in material conditions, the riddle capitalists have yet to solve.

Development of the productive forces can proceed without the capitalism, as we saw in the modernization of Russia, who went from constitutional monarchy and capitalism to socialism and put the first man and woman in space. China is experiencing similar development of the productive forces of industry, as the socialist model if nothing else generally is accompanied by massive industrial expansion, and growth of the natural sciences.

35

"The number of intellectuals who are hostile to our state is very small. They do not like our state, i.e., the dictatorship of the proletariat, and yearn for the old society. Whenever there is an opportunity, they will stir up trouble and attempt to overthrow the Communist Party and restore the old China. As between the proletarian and the bourgeois roads, as between the socialist and the capitalist roads, these people stubbornly choose to follow the latter. In fact, this road is impossible, and in fact, therefore, they are ready to capitulate to imperialism, feudalism and bureaucrat-capitalism. Such people are to be found in political circles and in industrial and commercial, cultural and educational, scientific, technological, and religious circles, and they are extremely reactionary.

-Ibid. pp. 3-4.

The unfortunate thing about the reactionary bourgeoisie is as in China they never go away even under a socialist state. All one has to do is look at the fall of the Soviet Union and one see the reforming of the bourgeoisie leading to Yeltsin and Putin. Indeed, the first was reactionary bourgeois, the latter bourgeois...

It is part of the experience to have the body on body struggle of modern society, inevitable in a bourgeois society, with ownership of the means of production in the hands of a few, with the majority of the society the proletariat.

"The serious problem is the education of the peasantry. The peasant economy is scattered, and the socialization of agriculture, judging by the Soviet Union's experience, will require a long time and painstaking work. Without socialization of agriculture, there can be no complete, consolidated socialism.

36

-"On the People's Democratic Dictatorship" June 30, 1949), Selected Works, Vol. IV, p. 419.

The sheer size of the population of China, as well as its large geographical size, presents a large task for the socialists. China has a population above 1 billion, and much of this is still on the land as it has been for thousands of years.

It should not simply be viewed from the 20th century perspective, a burden or embarrassment to be removed at the most convenient time. Rather the peasant must be the agent of change, building ecology and raising animals in a reasonable way, i.e. free ranging chickens vs. factory farmed animals. It is this China has, and the ecological work of planting the trees, turning the unused land in to coniferous forests, that the people on the land must set forward to do as their task.

The proletariat of the cities has the job of creating the heavy industry to build the terraces, with heavy machinery, to keep the hillsides from erosion.

The Soviets industrialized agriculture, and this model is compelling. The rapid industrialization occurred in all western societies, and in the case of America fundamentally altered the nature of the American dream. The workers now live in cities, and do not work the land.

This model can be helpful to China, but the ecological work must begin and where started, completed. Thus we see the peasant has a role to play, beyond simply farming food....

"We must have faith, first, that the peasant masses are ready to advance step by step along the road of socialism under the leadership of the Party, and second, that the Party is capable of leading the peasants along this road. These two points are the essence of the matter, the main current.

-On the Question of Agricultural Co-operation (July 31, 1955), 3rd ed., p. 18. *

The daunting task of revolutionizing the peasants, who are still in the developing world, is a recurring problem for socialism. Whether we like it or not in the industrialized world, China's people demand a high standard of living like the West. The problem becomes how to do this without irreparably damaging the ecology, and at the same time improve the material conditions of the workers.

The dominant model of industrial development at any cost is starting to shift. Renewable energy as opposed to nuclear is a case in point. Repeatedly the nuclear power advocates have said they create no atmospheric pollution causing global warming. This may seem to be true, but who wants to live downwind of a nuclear power plant? Obviously this type of industry causes atmospheric pollution, and no one really knows as of the 21st century exactly what small exposure to radiation causes as regards human health. It is still an abstraction, and its economic cost unknown…

Renewable energy such as wind and solar energy could raise the standard of living for China and if done properly could greatly help literacy in the countryside. The computer could become an indispensible part of life for China, eliminating the need for paper, bleached and mechanically pulped. It would also connect the peasant to the city, increasing the ability of the Communist Party to reach the desolate regions of China.

"The leading bodies in co-operatives must establish the dominant position of the poor peasants and the new lower middle peasants in these bodies, with the old lower middle peasants and the upper middle peasants - whether old or new - as the supplementary force. Only thus can unity between the poor and middle peasants be attained. Moreover, the co-operatives can also be consolidated, production can be expanded and the socialist transformation of the entire countryside be correctly accomplished in accordance with the Party's policy. Otherwise, unity between the middle and poor peasants cannot be attained, the co-operatives cannot be consolidated, production cannot be expanded, and the socialist transformation of the entire countryside cannot be achieved.

-Introductory note to "How Control of the Wutang Co-operative Shifted from the Middle to the Poor Peasants" (1955), The Socialist Upsurge in China's Countryside, Chinese ed., Vol. II.

Land reform, undertaken by the workers on the land, through cooperatives is a compelling idea. The presence of cooperatives, employee owned, could be the connection between the city and countryside needed to keep the path of China's industrial development socialist.

The presence of class in the countryside, especially in the western regions, continues to plague China. The separatist movement in Tibet, a country which only in the last 50 years ceased to be governed by a living god, the Dali Lama, mirrors the removal of the emperor accomplished after World War Two. But the Tibetan still craves the old ways, and finds support in the Western countries among the bourgeois for his attempts to slow modernization. Cooperatives may be the answer for the people here, with the help of the socialists to organize the peasants and provide the petroleum.

The Party must not be moved by bourgeois needs, rather stick to utility as the governing force, especially in Tibet, an old Asiatic society where material possessions are still viewed with suspicion. The recognition that all wealth is labour must be brought forward through literacy programmes for the workers. It is only this way the peasant will revolutionize the countryside, and the utility of objects recognized, and then beauty…

"It is essential to unite with the middle peasants, and it is wrong not to do so. But on whom must the working class and the Communist Party rely in the countryside in order to unite with the middle peasants and realize the socialist transformation of the entire countryside? Surely on none other than the poor peasants. That was the case when the struggle against the landlords was being waged and the land reform was being carried out, and that is the case today when the struggle against the rich peasants and other capitalist elements is being waged to achieve the socialist transformation of agriculture. In both these revolutionary periods, the middle peasants wavered in the initial stages. It is only after they clearly see the general trend of events and the approaching triumph of the revolution that the middle peasants will come in on the side of the revolution. The poor peasants must work on the middle peasants and win them over, so that the revolution will broaden from day to day until final victory.

-Introductory note to "The Lesson of the 'Middle-Peasant Cooperative' and the 'Poor-Peasant Co-operative' in Fuan County" (1955), The Socialist Upsurge in China's Countryside, Chinese ed., Vol. II.

Helping the poor peasants of China may seem to be out of the ability of the proletariat, as the socialist movement is dominated by the industrial worker. Nevertheless helping the peasant could be a greater focus for the western socialists. The best way for this to occur is trade with the industrialized countries, i.e. providing a bicycle with the expectation it will be used.

"The agricultural co-operative movement has been a severe ideological and political struggle from the very beginning. No cooperative can be established without going through such a struggle. Before a brand-new social system can be built on the site of the old, the site must be swept clean. Invariably, remnants of old ideas reflecting the old system remain in people's minds for a long time, and they do not easily give way. After a co-operative is established, it must go through many more struggles before it can be consolidated. Even then, the moment it relaxes its efforts it may collapse.

-Introductory note to "A Serious Lesson" (1955), The Socialist Upsurge in China's Countryside, Chinese ed., Vol. I.

Cooperatives rise and fall. Perhaps nationalization of the remnants of capitalism might also be a way of revolutionizing the countryside, as it obviously works in the city. The agricultural commune, with heavy industry, especially with the tractor, could be of assistance to the peasant. This method differs from cooperatives in that the power is in the hands of the state, controlled by the workers. It has teeth, as its representatives reside in the centers of power, and they can be very useful friends. In this way the nationalization of the farm can be achieved rather quickly. It is a method that must be considered as cooperatives are unfortunately weak when it comes to privatization…

"The spontaneous forces of capitalism have been steadily growing in the countryside in recent years, with new rich peasants springing up everywhere and many well-to-do middle peasants striving to become rich peasants. On the other hand, many poor peasants are still living in poverty for lack of sufficient means of production, with some in debt and others selling or renting out their land. If this tendency goes unchecked, the polarization in the countryside will inevitably be aggravated day by day. Those peasants who lose their land and those who remain in poverty will complain that we are doing nothing to save them from ruin or to help them overcome their difficulties. Nor will the well-to-do middle peasants who are heading in the capitalist direction be pleased with us, for we shall never be able to satisfy their demands unless we intend to take the capitalist road. Can the worker-peasant alliance continue to stand him in these circumstances? Obviously not! There is no solution to this problem except on a new basis. And that means to bring about, step by step, the socialist transformation of the whole of agriculture simultaneously with the gradual realization of socialist industrialization and the socialist transformation of handicrafts and capitalist industry and commerce; in other words, it means to carry out co-operation and eliminate the rich-peasant economy and the individual economy in the countryside so that all the rural people will become increasingly well off together. We maintain that this is the only way to consolidate the worker-peasant alliance.

-On the Question of Agricultural Co-operation (July 31, 1955), 3rd ed., pp. 26-27.*

The movement of the peasant of China has been one of great hardship, with ecological destruction causing environmental changes in agriculture, and desertification. Farming of the land for capitalists, in America, has caused many of the regions of the East of the country to become desert, and it is spreading with lakes drying up in the Carolinas, Georgia is unfarmable in most areas, and even the mountains of Tennessee drying up so much the rivers no longer flow. Undoubtedly China will only follow if allowed to become a capitalist agricultural power.

No one need be ashamed to be a peasant, the proletariat of Europe and America were also once peasants in the recent past. It is only through the industrial capitalist the proletariat was formed in the West, a relatively recent phenomenon. Ecological reconstruction and construction has to occur, with the proletariat running the heavy machinery, industrial labour, and the peasant planting the seeds and trees of the recovered countryside. This is the best way to eliminate the town country distinction.

"By over-all planning, we mean planning which takes into consideration the interests of the 600 million people of our country. In drawing up plans, handling affairs or thinking over problems, we must proceed from the fact that China has a population of 600 million people, and we must never forget this fact.

-On the Correct Handling of Contradictions Among the People (February 27, 1957), first pocket ed. p. 47.

The historical relevance of this cannot be stressed further. China had 600 million people in 1957, today about double that. The failure to plan for the future, and the ecological damage it has caused, is a problem for modern China. The one child policy must be continued, and the population controlled by the Party.

As previously mentioned, it is unlikely capitalism would have changed this any. India is also in the region, a capitalist state, and its population also exploded.

Expanding literacy efforts in the countryside would help this. Education of basic ecological principles, sustainable agriculture etc. would help put the train back on the tracks, and help the ecological conditions in the countryside. In the Western world a raise in the standard of living helped the population growth problem considerably. In many cases the population has not only stabilized, it is falling considerably, especially in Russia. In the latter case the capitalist government is directly encouraging people to have children, i.e. child bearing holidays, pointing to the success of socialism…

Chapter 5

Conditions of the Labourers

"After the countrywide victory of the Chinese revolution and the solution of the land problem, two basic contradictions will still exist in China. The first is internal, that is, the contradiction between the working class and the bourgeoisie. The second is external, which is the contradiction between China and the imperialist countries. Consequently, after the victory of the people's democratic revolution, the state power of the people's republic under the leadership of the working class must not be weakened but must be strengthened.

-"Report to the Second Plenary Session of the Seventh Central Committee of the Communist Party of China" (March 5, 1949), Selected Works, Vol. IV, p. 369.

The socialist revolution experiences the brunt of the capitalist onslaught. Universal suffrage, practiced in America for almost 36 years, with all people having a vote, including negroes who attained the vote at the late date of 1964, is still dominated by the bourgeoisie, although of late they have found a black capitalist named Barak Obama.

Oppression of the socialists, the brutal struggle of body on body between the classes, gives lie to the real conditions of the American Democratic Republic.

The corruption of democracy by oligarchial forces, a hallmark of the American system, where cash contributions to political leadership are allowed and encouraged, where the bourgeois control the purse strings of the leadership, is a factor leading to the rejection of the entire system.

In a state where the two parties name themselves Democrats and Republicans, and both support free trade, free markets, free enterprise and call this freedom, it should be no surprise the proletariat could be in favor of socialism. Both parties are capitalist, and gave the labourers a dictator in 2000 named George Bush, who lost the election by 500,000 votes. Further testing of the stomach of the proletariat could result in a collective vomit removing the capitalist parties altogether, and replacement of the bourgeois dictator next time with a socialist one...

"The People's democratic dictatorship is based on the alliance of the working class, the peasantry and the urban petty bourgeoisie, and mainly on the alliance of the workers and the peasants, because these two classes comprise 80 per cent of China's population. These two classes are the main force in overthrowing imperialism and the Kuomintang reactionaries. The transition from New Democracy to socialism also depends mainly upon their alliance.

-"On the People's Democratic Dictatorship" (June 30, 1949), Selected Works, Vol. IV, p. 421.

This aspect of the revolution is democratic: the 80 percent of the population are workers who socialism has helped. The overwhelming majority of society, in the western world closer to 90 percent, are proletarian, with the invention of the tractor, railroads, and recycling. This segment of society is currently ruled in America by the industrial bourgeoisie, as the aristocracy in the land was replaced by modern machinery and agribusiness. In China the peasants on the land all would seem to have benefited from socialism, although the move into cities of late and the growth of capital there has reformed a bourgeoisie who are the new exploiters.

It is unclear how the urban petty bourgeoisie in China could have supported Mao. In America this group is one of the worst examples of low wage labour, with restaurants in particular, employing minimum wage workers for well more than 40 hours a week, and always a greater than 8 hour day. This abuse of the proletariat is supported by the leadership's constant calls not to spend the states money to help the poor, and any time democratic activity such as petitions for sick leave is mentioned this group holds down the labourers, as they are in precarious position. In this respect the petty bourgeois in America are among the more reactionary of the bourgeoisie, and their position as middle class necessitates their acceptance of the big bourgeoisie, they have to take part in the party system,

Thus their support is a strange occurrence, and due to the national conditions in China.

The workers cannot always be expected to have unity and support the revolutionary labourers. The intrigues of the lumpen proletariat show this. What exactly is the motivation for the activities of this group? The community of women supported by them, the brothel, is obviously organized capitalistically.

When one views the lumpen proletariat generally all the activities that place them in society are capitalist activity, i.e. drug dealing. Thus there is no real guarantee all the workers have unity regarding the abolition of private property. In this respect we see the need for a dictatorship of the proletariat, as these groups cannot be trusted.

"Class struggle, the struggle for production and scientific experiment are the three great revolutionary movements for building a mighty socialist country. These movements are a sure guarantee that Communists will be free from bureaucracy and immune against revisionism and dogmatism, and will forever remain invincible. They are a reliable guarantee that the proletariat will be able to unite with the broad working masses and realize a democratic dictatorship. If, in the absence of these movements, the landlords, rich peasants, counterrevolutionaries, bad elements and monsters were all allowed to crawl out, while our cadres were to shut their eyes to all this and in many cases fail even to differentiate between the enemy and ourselves but were to collaborate with the enemy and were corrupted, divided and demoralized by him, if our cadres were thus pulled out or the enemy were able to sneak in, and if many of our workers, peasants, and intellectuals were left defenseless against both the soft and the hard tactics of the enemy, then it would not take long, perhaps only several years or a decade, or several decades at most, before a counterrevolutionary restoration on a national scale inevitably occurred, the Marxist-Leninist party would undoubtedly become a revisionist party or a fascist party, and the whole of China would change its color.

-Note on "The Seven Well-Written Documents of Chekiang Province Concerning Cadres' Participation in Physical Labour" (May 9, 1963), quoted in On Khrushchev's Phony Communism and Its Historical Lessons for the World, pp. 71-72. *

The realization of the inevitability of communism would seem to be in question here. Nevertheless it is true; the Communist Party can be corrupted by the desire for surplus value, i.e. the Soviet Union. We would be blind not to suggest there were elements in the European socialist movement who were corrupted by the desire for power, and later monetary incentives for their labour or lack of.

If experience teaches us anything it is the worst abuses of capitalists can return with a vengeance the minute defenses are let down, and capital is allowed to reform and the bourgeois to flourish.

The growth of fascism, nominally National Socialism, really supporters of the Reformation and the Catholics, should show us there are those who will blatantly lie to their people and refer to themselves as friends of the workers when they are the most reactionary elements in society. Do not be fooled, there is no communism in "national socialism".

The end of the socialist revolution lately seems to accompany the inheritance of power through a family, i.e. North Korea. As should be obvious this is no longer socialism, it is something else, more similar to the Western capitalists, i.e. the Bush family. It may not be fascism yet but it is sliding backwards.

China left behind familial dictatorship in the 20th century with the fall of the Emperor. George Bush II, son of George Bush I, in America took power without Universal Suffrage as his sanction, and he was quite capitalist. America could learn form China in this respect…

"Under the leadership of the Communist Party, the Chinese people are carrying out a vigorous rectification movement in order to bring about the rapid development of socialism in China on a firmer basis. It is a movement for carrying out a nation-wide debate which is both guided and free, a debate in the city and the countryside on such questions as the socialist road versus the capitalist road, the basic system of the state and its major policies, the working style of Party and government functionaries, and the question of the welfare of the people, a debate which is conducted by setting forth facts and reasoning things out, so as correctly to resolve those actual contradictions among the people which demand immediate solution. This is a socialist movement for the self-education and self-remolding of the people.

-"Speech at the Meeting of the Supreme Soviet of the USSR in Celebration of the 40th Anniversary of the Great October Socialist Revolution" (November 6, 1957)

Socialism does not occur without a debate, this we see Karl Marx's humble beginnings as a writer defending free speech in Germany. The need for free speech is a driving force in socialism, and must be allowed, even if the ideas are offensive.

There are limits to speech, i.e. incitement of racial hatred, that have no place in society and thus should be granted no medium. But there are discussions on industry, for example going metric in America, that must be debated. In this respect it is important to allow for an opposition.

Of course, in the latter case we see bourgeois free speech is quite restricted. Their literacy programmes must also come into question here, where the average person cannot even tell what temperature it is outside in Celsius. How a University can profess to be a center of free speech in the American Democratic Republic in the 2000's and still teach non metrically begs a real discussion...

" *Most arduous tasks lie ahead of us in the great work of construction. Although there are over 10 million members in our Party, they still constitute a very small minority of the country's population. In government departments and public organizations and enterprises, much work has to be done by non-Party people. It is impossible to get this work well done unless we are good at relying on the masses and co-operating with non-Party people. While continuing to strengthen the unity of the whole Party, we must also continue to strengthen the unity of all our nationalities, democratic classes, democratic parties and people's organizations, and to consolidate and expand the people's democratic united front, and we must conscientiously get rid of every unhealthy manifestation in any link in our work that is detrimental to the unity between the Party and the people.*

-"Opening Address at the Eighth National Congress of the Communist Party of China" (September 15, 1956).

This is of note to point out the party was numerically small in China in 1956. With only about 10 million members and a population of 600 million or more it is a testament to the ability of a small group of people with vision to greatly raise the standard of literacy and material conditions of a people in a small amount of time.

China has sent men into space, and produces many commodities today, under the leadership of this same Communist Party. Party membership has increased considerably, but is still numerically small compared to the population size.

Nevertheless respect for the desire or non desire to take part in political activities is a basic right, and must be tolerated…

Chapter 6

Political Economic Conditions

"...Qualitatively different contradictions can only be resolved by qualitatively different methods. For instance, the contradiction between the proletariat and the bourgeoisie is resolved by the method of socialist revolution; the contradiction between the great masses of the people and the feudal system is resolved by the method of democratic revolution; the contradiction between the colonies and imperialism is resolved by the method of national revolutionary war; the contradiction between the working class and the peasant class in socialist society is resolved by the method of collectivization and mechanization in agriculture; contradiction within the Communist Party is resolved by the method of criticism and self-criticism; the contradiction between society and nature is resolved by the method of developing the productive forces. . . . The principle of using different methods to resolve different contradictions is one that Marxist-Leninists must strictly observe.

-"On Contradiction" (August 1937), Selected Works, Vol. I, pp. 321-22.

Democratic revolutions occur during the fall of feudalism, when the development of the productive forces come into conflict with existing property relations; in particular industry such as the Power Loom, which rocked Europe's foundations in the 18th century. The fetters placed by aristocracy was overthrown, but the revolution was by no means over. Rather, a new stage was opened, where increasingly the conflict was the result of the antagonistic forces of capital and labour.

This sharpened the class struggle, and the continued advancement of industry further increased the division between bourgeois and labourer.

The democratic revolution made the feudal royalty a cost of production, and obviously unprofitable costs are eliminated by capital in short order. Thus we see the beheading of King Charles and his monarchy in France in 1789…

The socialist revolution progresses from this point, thus we see France as the center of the class struggle in the 19th century, eventually culminating in the overthrow of capitalism with the Paris Commune, an experiment never before tired, the complete abolition of private property.

It should be remembered capital is a pre socialist economic condition, and socialist ideas are not the "old government", even in the now capitalist Eastern Europe. The "old government" here is the forces of capital, harnessed by Adolf Hitler to attack the growth of socialism in the Soviet Union. The latter was a new force in society, that was no longer capitalistic, and were attempting to abolish private property.

Thus we see an emergence of China as a democratic revolution, as the overthrow of feudalism is often referred to as democratic. In reality, universal suffrage for all people in a culture can take hundreds of years to form, i.e. negroes being first allowed the vote in 1964 in America. It is also very easily overthrown by the bourgeoisie, for example George Bush II in 2000 when he lost the popular vote and yet still governed.

In this case we see the need for socialism, where the universal suffrage is overthrown already. It would not be a far cry to suggest a socialist dictatorship would have been preferable to the dictatorship of George

Bush II, who dragged the country into two long wars over buildings being bombed that were not even physically producing commodities.

Socialism generally cannot progress with a monarchy. Not only does the monarchy refuse to govern, as was the case in Russia with the Romanovs Nicholas and Alexander, as they are not in favor of by the people; revolution often removes them, as was also the case of the latter as well as with the emperor and the Forbidden City in China.

In some cases capitalism can be partially responsible for removal of monarchy, as in the Greek capitalist dictatorship in the 20th century when the king left the country. Of course, with the restoration of universal suffrage the return of the king became again an issue. The democratic socialists, the Pan Hellenic Socialist Movement (PASOK) who took power after dictatorship, put the measure to the vote in a referendum. The king lost, and feudalism in Greece was overthrown. Incidentally the PASOK again won the sanction of universal suffrage in 2009, and formed a government under George Papandreou. The victory of the socialists in Greece was a long struggle, and shows the ability of the democratic socialists effectively move the people down a more revolutionary path without violence.

The bourgeoisie still exists though, and is far from conquered in Greece. Rather, they have been dealt a blow, and must not be allowed to simply regroup and again promote production for surplus value. Furthermore Greece may have islands, but the majority of Greece is firmly attached to Europe. Thus forces of capital are capable of reaching Greece from elsewhere on the continent. Thus the revolution is still beginning…

"The only way to settle questions of an ideological nature or controversial issues among the people is by the democratic method, the method of discussion, of criticism, of persuasion and education, and not

by the method of coercion or repression. To be able to carry on their production and studies effectively and to arrange their lives properly, the people want their government and those in charge of production and of cultural and educational organizations to issue appropriate orders of an obligatory nature. It is common sense that the maintenance of public order would be impossible without such administrative regulations. Administrative orders and the method of persuasion and education complement each other in resolving contradictions among the people. Even administrative regulations for the maintenance of public order must be accompanied by persuasion and education, for in many cases regulations alone will not work.

-On the Correct Handling of Contradictions Among the People (February 27, 1957), 1st pocket ed., pp. 11-12.

In most cases in the Western countries the power of argument is all the communists have. Education remains something paid for, out of reach to the proletariat due to cost, and dominated by those whose families can afford it. In their eyes their education in Ivy League institutions allows for them to suggest they have superior argument to that of the labourer. They use this justification for the division of labour, and comprise the bourgeois middle class, and big bourgeoisie in America.

But the socialists still have the power of argument. The bourgeoisie is running on Adam Smith, the old ideas of supply and demand, and this must be logically approached by the socialists. With the writings of Karl Marx the questions of the old ideas of private property and the new ideas of communism dawn on society. No longer is the labourer in the dark clutching for morality, the ideas of the modern world now light him, a scientific dialectical materialism forms to guide forward the movement.

The continued progression of Marxism though inevitably leads to acceptance of naturalism, ecological ideas, as equality eventually begins to reach out to even non human members of society. Recognition of the ecological consequences of capital push the socialists away from an anthropocentric model, and modern technology i.e. recycling becomes the domain of the proletariat.

Here we see the power of argument in play, as the revolution says planting the trees is right, and capitalists say it is too expensive. But the argument remains, and even the bourgeoisie must admit it is right to try to fix the ecology. At this point they are capable of being defeated by nationalization of the ecological industries, i.e. recycling. In this respect ecological industry has been able to produce wealth for the labourer, a rarity that must be further developed...

Generally once the bourgeoisie discovers they are not going to win they become reclusive. They no longer listen to their labourers, and the stage of the struggle that includes attempts to isolate the intellectual begins.

The assessment of the labourer as hostile eventually can lead to the brutal struggle of body on body, due to the bourgeois recognition they are not winning the argument of communism. Thus marks a new stage of revolution...

"In ordinary circumstances, contradictions among the people are not antagonistic. However, if they are not handled properly, or if we relax our vigilance and lower our guard, antagonism may arise. In a socialist country, a development of this kind is usually only a localized and temporary phenomenon. The reason is that the system of exploitation of man by man has been abolished and the interests of the people are the same.

-On the Correct Handling of Contradictions Among the People (February 27, 1957), 1st pocket ed., p. 14.

Relaxing of discipline towards literacy will result in the failure of the revolution, the labourer must never cease to constantly be in the vanguard of proletarian thought, and never become an unwitting agent of capital.

Later the entire ecology dawns as a field of a new form of equality, the Ecological Era begins. It is a break from the Modern Era, as Man vs. Ecology is finally addressed. It is the growth of natural sciences progressing, i.e. satellite maps of global warming, that fundamentally alter mans relationship to the ecology.

The fetter of man vs. man keeps society from changing to a new era. Petty arguments over anthropocentric concerns almost brought about total nuclear war, anthropocentric ideas of primitive god images vs. anthropocentric socialism, not yet in the Ecological Era, the conditions of a previous millennium. Eventually the reformation of old relationships occurred, a proletarian and an exploiting class returned to the Eastern half of Europe. But the question of communism was not yet solved; the old society was still not winning the arguments of the new philosophy against private property. Thus we see demoralization in the capitalist camp, and the need to constantly resort to violence to control the labourer. The battle was not yet won in the new millennium...

"Every Communist must grasp the truth; "Political power grows out of the barrel of a gun."

-"Problems of War and Strategy" (November 6, 1938), Selected Works, Vol. II, p. 224.

Well there may be truth to this in that in the 00's war was still alive and well, and the American Democratic Republic was waging it, in Iraq and Afghanistan.

Even with the fall of the Soviet Union, America still spent the same amount of money on military expenditures as it did in the 80's. Barak Obama spent more than George Bush on the military, the first thing he did after taking power, and aggressively waged war on Afghanistan.

Whether we like it or not, the bourgeoisie obviously agrees with this statement…

"As for the imperialist countries, we should unite with their peoples and strive to coexist peacefully with those countries, do business with them and prevent any possible war, but under no circumstances should we harbour any unrealistic notions about them.

-On the Correct Handling of Contradictions Among the People (February 27, 1957), 1st pocket ed., p. 75.

China has basically adhered to this, trade with the imperialist countries. China is one of America's biggest trading partners, stores, i.e. Wal Mart sell a great variety of Chinese goods, and are present in virtually all of the country. It seems even the small towns have Wal Mart's now, an example of the trading relationship China enjoys with America.

But China must not adhere to illusions. Clearly the bourgeoisie exists in America, and is still attempting to aggressively expand its control over the world market. In this respect China should use caution in how they befriend countries who obviously oppress their labourer, and approach all protests and strikes with the baton and shield, i.e. the Pittsburgh G8 protests of 2009.

" Political work is the life-blood of all economic work. This is particularly true at a time when the social and economic system is undergoing fundamental change.

-Introductory note to "A Serious Lesson" (1955), The Socialist Upsurge in China's Countryside, Chinese ed., Vol. I.

Political economy nominally suggests the political nature of the economic structure of modern society. Economics and politics are connected as follows: Politics are spokes of the bicycle wheel, economics the hub and axel. Disconnection of the spokes makes the wheel fail...

The other spokes, philosophy, natural science, etc. are all essential to the functioning of the wheel, but all revolve around the economic structure of society. In this respect labour and production comprise the main focus of the movement, and dialectical materialism reflects this.

Historical materialism teaches us the position of the economic structure of society is a given point in history, and the material conditions accompanying it a reflection of the development of the productive forces.

"Things develop ceaselessly. It is only forty-five years since the Revolution of 1911, but the face of China has completely changed. In another forty-five years, that is, in the year 2001, or the beginning of the 21st century, China will have undergone an even greater change. She will have become a powerful socialist industrial country. And that is as it should be. China is a land with an area of 9,600,000 square kilometers and a population of 600 million people, and she ought to have made a greater contribution to humanity. Her contribution over a long period has been far too small. For this we are regretful. But we must be modest - not only now, but forty-five years hence as well. We should always be modest. In our international relations, we Chinese people should get rid of great-power chauvinism resolutely, thoroughly, wholly and completely.

-"In Commemoration of Dr. Sun Yat-sen" (November 1956).

Amazing how Mao's prediction could have been so true! China indeed became a world power, and its production was par excellence in 2001. Chinese commodities were made cheaply and effectively, and on sale throughout America in 2001.

China even to this date escaped the recession that set in in the late 00's, when Japan and America declined as world powers.

If Mao had said 100 years ago China would be a power in production rivaling Western Europe and America in the near future he would have been laughed out of the room. This attests to the victory of socialism in China. But there is still more to do. Ecological revolution must occur; the hillsides terraced, the desert fought with the same vigor the bourgeoisie was countered with in the 20th century. The beginnings of this was evident recently in China's decision to plant trees in an area the size of Norway in China. These developments are favorable to the growth of the proletariat, and will serve as a monument to revolutionary socialist progress well into the new millennium.

Chapter 7

Dialectical Materialism

"In their social practice, men engage in various kinds of struggle and gain rich experience, both from their successes and from their failures. Countless phenomena of the objective external world are reflected in a man's brain through his five sense organs - the organs of sight, hearing, smell, taste and touch. At first, knowledge is perceptual. The leap to conceptual knowledge, i e., to ideas, occurs when sufficient perceptual knowledge is accumulated. This is one process in cognition. It is the first stage in the whole process of cognition, the stage leading from objective matter to subjective consciousness, from existence to ideas. Whether or not one's consciousness or ideas (including theories, policies, plans or measures) do correctly reflect the laws of the objective external world is not yet proved at this stage, in which it is not yet possible to ascertain whether they are correct or not. Then comes the second stage in the process of cognition, the stage leading from consciousness back to matter, from ideas back to existence, in which the knowledge gained in the first stage is applied in social practice to ascertain whether the theories, policies, plans or measures meet with the anticipated success. Generally speaking, those that succeed are correct and those that fail are incorrect, and this is especially true of man's struggle with nature. In social struggle, the forces representing the advanced class sometimes suffer defeat not because their ideas are incorrect but because, in the balance of forces engaged in struggle, they are not as powerful for the time being as the forces of reaction; they are therefore temporarily defeated, but they are bound to triumph sooner or later. Man's knowledge makes another leap through the test of practice. This leap is more important than the previous one. For it is this leap alone that can prove the correctness or incorrectness of the first leap in cognition, i.e., of the ideas, theories, policies, plans or measures formulated in the

course of reflecting the objective external world. There is no other way of testing truth.

-Where Do Correct Ideas Come from? (May 1963), pp. 1-3

The conditions of the objective world allow for the abstraction of the subjective; they condition the ideas and thoughts of the human being, they form the basis of language, and the lions share of language is directly related to the material world.   This becomes obvious when dealing with machinery, i.e. the automobile and its parts, there are thousands of words attached the aspects of the motor, developed through application of the natural sciences.

It is through the medium of material mankind expresses his most profound thoughts, books, music, etc. all on paper and later as this book on a computer.

Prior to the revolution of the written word there was lyrical poetry, i.e. Homer, which guided man in his morality and religion. Indeed mans oldest writings are theology, passed down as poetry and song for many years.

But Plato, Aristotle, Herodotus, Thucydides used the written word, a far more precise method of transmitting ideas. These philosophers and historians set the events occurring around them into text, and profoundly affected the modern world. We read the word as it was then, with only a translation to English.

Thus we see the material aspect of knowledge, requiring paper and pen.

Later in the new millennium we see the computer allowing for instant access to encyclopedia, and the ability to purchase and read books not available previously. The computer is a sophisticated instrument for writing. In this respect we see the moral force of modern industry, a device that allows for international communication as well as well as advanced writing. The thoughts of the historical epoch are intimately connected to the material conditions of a culture.

"If a man wants to succeed in his work, that is, to achieve the anticipated results, he must bring his ideas into correspondence with the laws of the objective external world; if they do not correspond, he will fail in his practice. After he fails, he draws his lessons, corrects his ideas to make them correspond to the laws of the external world, and can thus turn failure into success; this is what is meant by "failure is the mother of success" and "a fall into the pit, a gain in your wit".

-"On Practice" (July 1937), Selected Works, Vol. I, pp. 296-97.

This statement echoes other statements by Mao in that defeat teaches us valuable lessons, and should be expected. Failure teaches one to be humble, and allows one to see the often hidden hand of the bourgeois. In this respect failure is an accomplishment, and respected as good intentions if it was indeed for this.

The many unsuccessful attempts to make revolution, often resulting in violence against the proletariat are an embarrassment to the upper classes. To have to use violent means to control ones own countryman, who approaches with or without violence, the latter being most often the case, is the most embarrassing moment in running a government, and is the main factor leading to its failure. When the hidden hand is seen, i.e. Hitler's SS, on the brink of failure leading to desperation, and increasingly violent efforts to stop the labourer from emancipation from the bonds of surplus value, we see the real nature of the bourgeois. It is crude, direct, and violent. This marks the true progress of the Modern Era, the ability to see and understand the real methods of social control practiced by class society, especially capitalism in the historical epoch of private property and the world market.

"The analytical method is dialectical. By analysis, we mean analyzing the contradictions in things. And sound analysis is impossible without intimate knowledge of life and without real understanding of the pertinent contradictions.

-Speech at the Chinese Communist Party's National Conference on Propaganda Work (March 12, 1957), l5t pocket ed., and p. 20.

The essence of the Marxist philosophy is dialectical. It literally is dialectic; it is the spoken word. It ideas are gained through repeated debate, especially with the opposition, as capitalists predate the communist movement.

Indeed all secrets of communists are the secrets of the bourgeois. The only secrets communists hold is a desire to remove the bourgeoisie, and the method of so doing, which obviously do not stay a secret long once ideas are put in motion.

The method of analysis, dialectical, is the essence of the movement towards free speech.

The contradictions in things, i.e. their presence as an object labored on in the objective sense, compared to their utility or beauty as a statement of status, marks the historical nature of the object in question. Competition produces the desire to lower labour costs, and the ultimate source of cheap labour is always prison. Thus the subjective essence becomes important to the proletariat, an object produced right gains a greater meaning than mere possession. It is labour, and this is the true reflection of the value of the commodity to the labourer...

"Natural science is one of man's weapons in his fight for freedom. For the purpose of attaining freedom in society, man must use social science to understand and change society and carry out social revolution. For the purpose of attaining freedom in the world of nature, man must use natural science to understand, conquer and change nature and thus attain freedom from nature.

-Speech at the inaugural meeting of the Natural Science Research Society of the Border Region (February 5, 1940).

With all due respect to the constant struggle of man and environment, and recognizing the hostility of man to ecology as an historical fact, this idea must be critiqued.

Clearly conquering nature is a 2nd millennium thought, which does not fit with naturalism. These ideas of conquering nature have cost China's ecology greatly. They led to a population explosion, and environmental pollution persistent into the new millennium.

It is time the Marxists faced up to the fact ecology deserves respect, and this is a form of equality. Just because something has no language does not mean mankind has the right to destroy it...

This is the idea of conquering nature, to harness the ecology for anthropocentric gain.

A new millennium dawns. Ecology should not be conquered, it should be cooperated with. A paradigm shift is occurring, and man is increasingly having to weigh ecology when constructing industry or habitating an area.

In all fairness capitalism destroyed the ecology in the west as bad as China. Logging rainforests, the pollution of water supplies by factories, etc. all took place under private property.

It is sincerely hoped China will show communism is compatible with the ecology, and undertake reforestation, end nuclear power production, and create a comprehensive recycling programme. This is not outside their ability, and is a historically new idea, something they could enjoy embracing…

"The Marxist philosophy of dialectical materialism has two outstanding characteristics. One is its class nature: it openly avows that dialectical materialism is in the service of the proletariat. The other is its practicality: it emphasizes the dependence of theory on practice, emphasizes that theory is based on practice and in turn serves practice.

-"On Practice" (July 1937), Selected Works, Vol. I, p. 297.

This is correct; the dialectical materialism is in the service of the proletariat. Previously political economy before Karl Marx was all businessmen. No one approached political economy from the perspective of the labourer, it was always from the perspective of the private property owner.

What differentiates Marxism is it is political economy explained through the eyes of the proletariat. Dialectical materialism is political economy for the labourer. It service is to the people who do not own private property, rather labour for their pay, and do not own the means of production.

Its relationship to naturalism is it sees concrete objective conditions as being caused by man as well as ecology. It connects man to the subjective, as a creator of his own destiny, as opposed to the externalization. In this respect we see Marxism as totally in agreement with naturalism, even recognizing the instinct in man to be social, an advancement from the Robinson Caruso abstractions of the early political economists.

"It is man's social being that determines his thinking. Once the correct ideas characteristic of the advanced class are grasped by the masses, these ideas turn into a material force which changes society and changes the world.

-Where Do Correct Ideas Come from? (May 1963), 1st pocket ed., p. 1.

The understanding of this is crucial, the idea social culture causes the dominant paradigm in society. The masses respond with distrust when they feel they have been taken, and as the majority of society is proletarian, this force becomes unstoppable even when the masses have little real economic power, as they do not control the production process.

The importance of constant efforts to reach the masses through reading and writing is of importance to every Marxist. It is his job to continually attempt to emancipate the labourer through revolutionary study, and accept the suffering of the proletariat as a member of them.

The middle class is not the revolutionary class, although they may be more literate than the labourer. The Marxist must accept his position as labour, and not join the bourgeoisie, or its middle class sympathizers.

The material forces of production must be understood, and a conscious effort made to control them, especially through nationalization. This comes from the revolutionary class, and although it may resemble desperate tactics to bail out companies, or otherwise good intentions from the bourgeoisie, the labourer is the ultimate holder of the destiny of the productive forces.

If the factory is nationalized due to economic conditions unfavorable to capitalism, the labourer must stand up for himself and maintain the shift away from private property. If he does not the factory will revert to capital, and surplus value will return. It is only through constant effort the factory in the non private property form can be maintained.

"Whoever wants to know a thing has no way of doing so except by coming into contact with it, that is, by living (practicing) in its environment. ... If you want knowledge, you must take part in the practice of changing reality. If you want to know the taste of a pear, you must change the pear by eating it yourself.... If you want to know the theory and methods of revolution, you must take part in revolution. All genuine knowledge originates in direct experience.

-"On Practice" (July 1937), Selected Works, Vol. I, pp. 299-300.

It is through the revolutionary experience of being on the opposite end of the weapon that hones the revolutionary and makes him fit to govern. Bureaucratic rising through the ranks has no place in a real revolution. A real revolution is not a dinner party, it is a long and bloody experience when there are days you remain committed to the end but sometimes feel it is pointless. Then consciousness kicks in and the socialist movement becomes worth the effort.

Emancipation of the proletariat from the bonds of surplus value! The rallying cry of all communists.

Only through real suffering can the labourer ever hope to emancipate himself and his fellow labourers from the oppressive relationship of capital to labour.

Only the Marxist sees the bourgeois hand clearly, and only he is fit to govern the masses, as he understands the oppression the bourgeois is capable of dishing out. His experience, oppressed, alone, isolated and violently attacked repeatedly, often by the lumpen proletariat, whose service to the bourgeois remain a subject of intrigue, conditions the character of the proletariat, and it is the real education to lead.

In revolutions where the proletariat has already gained power, such as in China, the experience of dealing with the other territories, i.e. Taiwan, Japan, hone the skills of the revolutionary. The constant contact with the oppressed labourer of these societies and the goal of emancipation shared by both must be the torch that leads the people.

Revolution does not end after the proletariat gains power; it is a dynamic ever changing set of challenges to continue to remain on the vanguard of proletarian thought and to put these ideas into practice.

"Knowledge begins with practice, and theoretical knowledge, which is acquired through practice, must then return to practice. The active function of knowledge manifests itself not only in the active leap from perceptual to rational knowledge, but - and this is more important - it must manifest itself in the leap from rational knowledge to revolutionary practice.

-Ibid. p. 304.*

Application of Marxism to the national conditions of society, differing from country to country, some more or less developed, is revolutionary practice. Marxism is still revolutionary in all parts of the world, especially with the unprecedented growth of the world market, crowning achievement of capitalism.

In Eastern Europe the anthropocentric socialist model has fallen, leaving behind economic crisis and constant attempts to prop up the countries who seceded from the Soviet Union with massive loans from the west. Whether or not they can pay is something still being discussed. It would seem capitalism reformed and now is ruling most of the industrialized world.

Is there still fertile ground for Marxism? We must answer yes.

The quest for surplus value from in Eastern Europe has lowered the standard of living for the average European. They have become less literate, and the old crotchets of Christian ideology returned. They are in an oppressed condition now, economic crisis slowing eating away at society, the result of the application of capitalist ideas to their cultures.

It is prime time for some revolutionary practice learned through the observation of what capitalism has brought the last 20 years in the old Soviet Union. The labourer now produces surplus value; reform of the bourgeois only strengthened the grip of capital over a people who were once free of man exploiting man.

The entire thing rests on the shoulders of the labourers, who must be the bearer of the new banner of ecological socialism through revolutionary practice.

"The most fundamental method of work, which all Communists must firmly bear in mind, is to determine our working policies according to actual conditions. When we study the causes of the mistakes we have made, we find that they all arose because we departed from the actual situation at a given time and place and were subjective in determining our working policies.

-"Speech at a Conference of Cadres in the Shansi-Suiyuan Liberated Area" (April 1, 1948), Selected Works, Vol. IV, pp. 229-30. *

It is essential to understand the subjective and objective conditions of people are not always identical.

The most obvious instance of this is the more industrialized countries and the less.

It is in this way we see the national conditions of people often to be quite different. It is not unrealistic to consider the same programme for socialism would not work in both societies, subjectively or objectively....

" When we look at a thing, we must examine its essence and treat its appearance merely as an usher at the threshold, and once we cross the threshold, we must grasp the essence of the thing; this is the only reliable and scientific method of analysis.

-"A Single Spark Can Start a Prairie Fire" (January 5, 1930), Selected Works, Vol. I, p. 119.

A things appearance may determine its use value as a commodity, and similarly even help determine its exchange value. Of course, subjectively the thing can have an entirely different value, i.e. a tomato grown in the garden and one bought at the store. The tomato grown in the garden may be of higher quality, it does not sit on the shelf, but really it is not all that much different than one bought in a good market. It is the act of labour that determines the things worth, it has the same use value but it is even beyond exchange value. Its exchange value is low; it is not worth much more than a regular tomato at the store. If we were to ascribe an exchange value to the object, we would be unable to ask for even twice as much as a regular tomato. This is because of the subjective essence of wealth. The tomato has a value beyond exchange value because of the labour required to produce it. Its subjective essence is that of a personal effort, and its existence as an object has meaning beyond the commodity bought at the store.

The subjective essence of an object is lost to capitalists, who are only attached to an object for exchange value. Their view of the labour process is to create surplus value, and beyond this there is only the power of the state inspector to stop child labour, make them pay health care costs, etc. The subjective essence of the object is lost, and the expansion of the world market further loses the identity of the object. In many cases one does not even know the country the object is produced in, i.e. automobile parts produced in less developed countries.

In this respect we see the subjective nature of the object, a product of labour, having a different identity although the object is virtually the same. It is the moral force of the object, it has meaning of how it was produced, and is not simply an exchange value. Its essence is that of a thing laboured on, and the act of labour determines the subjective essence of the object.

"Marxist philosophy holds that the law of the unity of opposites is the fundamental law of the universe. This law operates universally, whether in the natural world, in human society, or in man's thinking. Between the opposites in a contradiction there is at once unity and struggle, and it is this that impels things to move and change. Contradictions exist everywhere, but they differ in accordance with the different nature of different things. In any given phenomenon or thing, the unity of opposites is conditional, temporary and transitory, and hence relative, whereas the struggle of opposites is absolute.

-On the Correct Handling of Contradictions Among the People (February 27, 1957), 1st pocket ed., p. 18.

The opposites in a thing are often historically defined, i.e. an engine in an automobile. When automobiles first made their appearance in the last century, it was liberation from the horse. The ability to get to the market without the horse was liberation for the horse as well as the human, the human no longer had to clean up after the animal, and the horse no longer had to stay chained in the stable.

Unfortunately as time passed and hundreds of millions of automobiles had been produced the climate began to change from the amount of petroleum burned. Furthermore people became chained to the material thing the automobile; they needed it to get to work. There was the beginnings of movements to use bicycles and mass transit (trains, buses etc.) to help the ecology.

Of course lost to most was the fact the automobile is just an engine driving four wheels. The same engine could be used to pump water to grow trees, or other useful purposes. The contradictoriness of the object, a motor driving four wheels, as opposed to a motor chained to a well, was the historical condition of the society.

The appropriation of the object for a purpose not beneficial to the labourer marks the historical position of development of a given object. It is due to the social conditions that the motor in the automobile example is wasteful. The motor is just a motor, it has no consciousness. It is not even a horse, it is simply a collection of metal and bolts. Yet in society it develops a meaning, and a socially acceptable use. It is not used as a motor to pump water due to social factors, rather it is transportation.

Liberation of the object is intimately connected to the labour process, as labour controlled by the bourgeoisie. The bourgeoisie in capitalist society determines what will be produced, and the conditions of labour. Even in China under communism the consumer habits of the capitalist societies determined the needs of the people. Bourgeois needs came to China, the labourer felt he really needed an automobile. And thus the struggle of the material object became evident even though the labour was in the process of liberation…

Chapter 8

Material Conditions of Production and Society

"While we recognize that in the general development of history the material determines the mental and social being determines social consciousness, we also - and indeed must - recognize the reaction of mental on material things, of social consciousness on social being and of the superstructure on the economic base. This does not go against materialism; on the contrary, it avoids mechanical materialism and firmly upholds dialectical materialism.

-"On Contradiction" (August 1937), Selected Works, Vol. I, p. 336. *

The historical development of culture has a material basis, it is the development of the productive forces. Of course, society often is not ready for the new industry, the struggles over the addition of the ribbon weaver in Europe of the 18th century are a prime example:

"The contest between the capitalist and the wage-labourer dates back to the very origin of capital. It raged on throughout the whole manufacturing period. But only since the introduction of machinery has the workman fought against the instrument of labour itself, the material embodiment of capital. He revolts against this particular form of the means of production, as being the material basis of the capitalist mode of production.

"In the 17th century nearly all Europe experienced revolts of the workpeople against the ribbon-loom, a machine for weaving ribbons and trimmings, called in Germany Bandmühle, Schnurmühle, and Mühlenstuhl. These machines were invented in Germany. Abbé Lancellotti, in a work that appeared in Venice in 1636, but which was written in 1579, says as follows:

""Anthony Müller of Danzig saw about 50 years ago in that town, a very ingenious machine, which weaves 4 to 6 pieces at once. But the Mayor being apprehensive that this invention might throw a large number of workmen on the streets, caused the inventor to be secretly strangled or drowned."

"In Leyden, this machine was not used till 1629; there the riots of the ribbon-weavers at length compelled the Town Council to prohibit it.

"In hac urbe," says Boxhorn (Inst. Pol., 1663), referring to the introduction of this machine into Leyden, "ante hos viginti circiter annos instrumentum quidam invenerunt textorium, quo solus plus panni et facilius conficere poterat, quan plures aequali tempore. Hinc turbae ortae et querulae textorum, tandemque usus hujus instrumenti a magistratu prohibitus est."

[In this town, about twenty years ago certain people invented an instrument for weaving , with which a single person could weave more cloth, and more easily, than many others in the same length of time. As a result there arose disturbances and complaints from the weavers, until the Town Council finally prohibited the use of this instrument.]

"After making various decrees more or less prohibitive against this loom in 1632, 1639, &c., the States General of Holland at length permitted it to be used, under certain conditions, by the decree of the 15th December, 1661. It was also prohibited in Cologne in 1676, at the same time that its introduction into England was causing disturbances among the workpeople. By an imperial Edict of 19th Feb., 1685, its use was forbidden throughout all Germany. In Hamburg it was burnt in public by order of the Senate. The Emperor Charles VI., on 9th Feb., 1719, renewed the edict of 1685, and not till 1765 was its use openly allowed in the Electorate of Saxony. This machine, which shook Europe to its foundations, was in fact the precursor of the mule and the power-loom, and of the industrial revolution of the 18th century. It enabled a totally inexperienced boy, to set the whole loom with all its shuttles in motion, by simply moving a rod backwards and forwards, and in its improved form produced from 40 to 50 pieces at once.

-Karl Marx Capital V.1 Section 5: Strife between Workman and Machine

By this example we see social conditions determining growth of the natural sciences. Clearly social phenomenon, in Mao's description "…the reaction of mental on material things, of social consciousness on social being and of the superstructure on the economic base." play a large role in the development of natural sciences and society. The banning of the loom shows social factors placing fetters on the development of the productive forces. This is due to the consciousness level of the culture at the given time.

Material conditions may give rise to the development of society, but society can hinder, as in the weaver example, the addition of new machinery due to fear of unrest.

Obviously putting the genie back in the bottle is also impossible, and eventually the new ribbon machine was adopted. Nevertheless there is a definite connection between the consciousness of a society and its material cultural development.

It resembles modern America and its struggle against the metric system. The fetters on the development of industry, to stop the growth of socialism, could not be more felt than in the 21st century. America remained the last country to do a metric conversion, even in the developing world. In many respects America was a member of the developing world, with antiquated pollution creating machinery only serviceable by American non metric factories.

The social conditions of man are created by him, otherwise we get externalization. Society does not miraculously move forward, sometimes it progresses in leaps and bounds, others it stagnates. If society did not stagnate empires would not rise and fall. We have seen repeatedly how massive advanced cultures can eventually be defeated, often by the less scientifically advanced, i.e. a metric Soviet Union and non metric America of the 20th century...

"Everyone engaged in practical work must investigate conditions at the lower levels. Such investigation is especially necessary for those who know theory but do not know the actual conditions, for otherwise they will not be able to link theory with practice. Although my assertion, "No investigation no right to speak", has been ridiculed as "narrow empiricism", to this day I do not regret having made it; far from regretting it, I still insist that without investigation there cannot possibly be any right to speak. There are many people who "the moment they alight from the official carriage" make a hullabaloo, spout opinions, criticize this and condemn that; but, in fact, ten out of ten of them will

meet with failure. For such views or criticisms, which are not based on thorough investigation, are nothing but ignorant twaddle. Countless times our Party suffered at the hands of these "imperial envoys", who rushed here, there and everywhere. Stalin rightly says "theory becomes purposeless if it is not connected with revolutionary practice". And he rightly adds that "practice gropes in the dark if its path is not illumined by revolutionary theory". Nobody should be labeled a "narrow empiricist" except the "practical man" who gropes in the dark and lacks perspective and foresight.

-"Preface and Postscript to Rural Surveys" (March and April 1941), Selected Works, Vol. III, p. 13. *

Nothing could possibly be more nauseating than having to hear the so called "educated" ideas of the bourgeoisie regarding socialism. Bred in universities, and other places of "higher culture" these tired ideas flourish. They are from people who only know the official line on life as a proletariat, who secretly dread having to live and associate with the labourers, and often refuse to associate with the proletarian.

Self taught ideas are far more powerful than the official teachings of the bourgeois who are well paid, and often their positions of professor makes them prime candidates for recruitment in to the offices of the government. There they take the positions of defining the ruling ideas of the institutions of American culture, and all their crotchets of superiority intellectually over the labourer are given full force by decree from their masters.

The best thoughts and ideas of the proletariat come through the real life experiences of the revolution. It teaches a man to accept defeat, that not all battles can be won.

Our bourgeoisie still clings to the idea they are invincible, and it is very demoralizing for them to lose a battle, i.e. Vietnam.

The proletariat understands defeat, learns from it, and patiently waits for the conditions to again continue to attempt to change society towards socialism. He sees the hand of the bourgeois, as it has oppressed him. He has no misgivings of harnessing capitalism, he is in the vanguard of the proletariat, and his life experience is what makes his ideas and theories truth.

"With victory, certain moods may grow within the Party - arrogance, the airs of a self-styled hero, inertia and unwillingness to make progress, love of pleasure and distaste for continued hard living. With victory, the people will be grateful to us and the bourgeoisie will come forward to flatter us. It has been proved that the enemy cannot conquer us by force of arms. However, the flattery of the bourgeoisie may conquer the weak-willed in our ranks. There may be some Communists, who were not conquered by enemies with guns and were worthy of the name of heroes for standing up to these enemies, but who cannot withstand sugar-coated bullets; they will be defeated by sugar-coated bullets. We must guard against such a situation.

-"Report to the Second Plenary Session of the Seventh Central Committee of the Communist Party of China" (March 5, 1949), Selected Works, Vol. IV, p. 374.

It is the story of the Soviet Union, where bourgeois needs triumphed over the desire to enjoy equality. The people began wanting blue jeans, cars, etc. They were no longer happy with what they had achieved without surplus value in production.

Many of them thought they could become wealthy, and the sugar coated bullets of the bourgeoisie conquered them. They became capitalists, and aggressively pushed the market on their previous equals.

Poverty returned, and the only real advancement of the society was a limited universal suffrage, minus the communist party who were often made illegal, such as when Yeltsin bombed parliament because the communists were in control of it.

Out of the frying pan and into the fire. The restricted conditions that brought about the bourgeois needs now brought poverty, and a lowered health among the labourers. Some people made large sums of money selling off the property once owned and produced by the proletariat. They gained power through this, and proceeded to attempt to completely conquer the workers state.

They found success and were still in power into the new millennium.

The remnants of socialism, nationalized industry, were still the target of the reformed bourgeoisie, and a democratic socialist party was yet to form. The people remembered the hard lives they had as a bulwark of socialism, and lost track of the fact their society was a new experiment. They began to call socialism an old system, and capitalism the new way. This was the beginning of the end. Western capitalists mercilessly attacked the workers state, calling the nationalized industry monopolies, the very thing socialism was reacting against, private property.

Finally the workers state broke. It had been deteriorating for some time since Joseph Stalin. The new leaders were increasingly from the bureaucracy, and had not had the revolutionary experience such as being sent to Siberia, which both Lenin and Stalin had experienced. They felt sorry for the collaborators with the Nazis, forgetting the 6 million soldiers from Western Europe's capitalism who marched in to Russia intent on destroying the workers state. Just what exactly to do with the millions of men who arrived to support the bourgeoisie with guns was lost to them, and they decried the prisoners at the labour camps and their treatment.

It was a horror of war to have to labour camp the Nazis, but one must remember they were not invited to socialist Russia. These men came with one goal: to stop socialism. They sealed their fate when they left the west of Europe to put down the proletariat with powder and lead...

"Liberalism is extremely harmful in a revolutionary collective. It is a corrosive which eats away unity, undermines cohesion, causes apathy and creates dissension. It robs the revolutionary ranks of compact organization and strict discipline, prevents policies from being carried through and alienates the Party organizations from the masses which the Party leads. It is an extremely bad tendency.

-"Combat Liberalism" (September 7, 1937), Selected Works, Vol. II,, p. 32.

Aristotle defined a Liberal as someone who is entrusted with a sum of money, by chance or inherited, does a good thing with it, so is rewarded by the community with more money.

The collective labourers have not access to large sums of money. The philanthropic wishes of the labourer may not be different from the philanthropist; the morality of the liberal are not always in question here. What is in question where the money comes from.

All wealth comes from labour, and fortunes are made through production for surplus value. The Liberal does not work, he cares for his fortune to accomplish his ends (in this case benevolent).

If he was laboring why he had large sums of money would be the natural next question, and where it came from. This leads to his membership in the bourgeoisie.

Creating jobs, stopping cruelty to animals, etc. are worthy goals, but the fact remains the fortunes spent come from the exploitation of the proletariat, and no good intention of giving can remove this ugly fact about the nature of wealth.

If this person wanted to really help the labourer he could simply give the money back to the exploited labourer at the factory, the origin of the surplus value. In this respect we see him as another bourgeois, nothing more than a money man, albeit with good intentions. It should be no surprise this persons removal is a goal of socialism...

"If we have shortcomings, we are not afraid to have them pointed out and criticized, because we serve the people. Anyone, no matter who, may point out our shortcomings. If he is right, we will correct them. If what he proposes will benefit the people, we will act upon it.

-"Serve the People" (September 8, 1941), Selected Works, Vol. III, P. 227.

The need for constant criticism is reflected in the Berlin Wall, when the opposition was cut off by the wall on both sides. One side became aggressively capitalist, and closed its ranks, the other side no longer had a means of communication openly and began to cease to have an opposition.

This eventually led to irreconcilable differences in Germany, and this remained for almost 50 years.

When the Berlin Wall came down the socialists adopted bourgeois needs, and the ideology of capitalists began to take hold. As most had been sheltered from the harshness of bourgeois society, they felt they were not being told the truth about the real nature of labour.

This sheltering from the constant criticism from capitalists led to the dissolution of the German Democratic Republic.

It is unclear exactly what the average proletarian German is thinking now. The opposition is where they now find themselves, to the ruling

Christian Democrats. Universal Suffrage has returned, an advancement, but bourgeois ideas are ruling the old German Democratic Republic. They would be wise to remain patient, learn from the old society and its idea, and prepare for the change to an ecological socialism, and the removal of the Christian Democrats, perhaps by Universal Suffrage.

Maintenance of Universal Suffrage should be continued until dictatorship of capitalists occurs. When the latter occurs we have a fertile ground for the dictatorship of the proletariat, there already is no Universal Suffrage, and an opposition in exile. Replacement of the capitalist dictator with a socialist must occur.

At some point Universal Suffrage may return, but first the reactionary bourgeoisie must be brought under control. This could take more or less time depending on national conditions. One thing is certain: the group of reaction is not going to be easily removed. Political violence could remove this bourgeoisie far faster than without war, returning the Universal Suffrage to the proletariat. A non violent revolution could take considerably longer to return Universal Suffrage, as simply returning the oppression experienced by the labourer under capitalism is no longer in favor...

"In order to build a great socialist society it is of the utmost importance to arouse the broad masses of women to join in productive activity. Men and women must receive equal pay for equal work in production. Genuine equality between the sexes can only be realized in the process of the socialist transformation of society as a whole.

-Introductory note to "Women Have Gone to the Labour Front" (1955), The Socialist Upsurge in China's Countryside, Chinese ed., Vol. I.

The ability of women to rise in the socialist hierarchy cannot be stressed further. The movement of women toward Universal Suffrage in America in the early years of the 20th century is parallel to the struggle for women's rights in China. In both cases the traditional role of women had to change; divorce eventually had to become more common, and the use of women as simply a source of cheap labour, i.e. the pretty ones as barmaid, stopped.

Women's Universal Suffrage in America helped give rise to Franklin Delano Roosevelt, who helped liberate China in the 40's. The fight against Japanese imperialism and support for Joseph Stalin led to the defeat of the reactionary bourgeoisie in Japan.

The revolutionary female proletariat in America if failing because many do not see equality and socialism as worthy goals anymore, they have bourgeois needs, and desire to climb in the capitalist hierarchy, where they become middle class or join the bourgeoisie.

Nevertheless the goal of equality for women remains; and the ability of women to vote is a form of equality. We must remember Chinese communism came in many ways from the fight against imperialism, from fighting the Chinese bourgeoisie, and the Japanese imperialists. In this respect equality in China has been progressing remarkably, and although the leadership seems to be slipping back into capitalism, there is still progress towards more rights for women.

At some point a female leader for China would seem to be in order, Whether or not she is sanctioned by Universal Suffrage is not as important as her ability to lead, to have vision of an ecological socialist society, and bring China forward.

" Enable every woman who can work to take her place on the labour front, under the principle of equal pay for equal work. This should be done as quickly as possible.

-Introductory note to "On Widening the Scope of Women's Work in the Agricultural Co-operative Movement" (1955), The Socialist Upsurge in China's Countryside, Chinese ed., Vol. I.

Equal pay for equal work is simplistic but a good plan. Empowering women to be mens equals is only possible if they are not simply a source of cheap labour, rather a proletariat capable of leadership.

For many years women have been treated as property by men, in America in particular. It was only in the last century divorce became acceptable, liberating women from the bondage of male dominance.

With equal pay for equal work women should be able to create equality in China for their sex in short order. It is one of the glaring inequalities in Western culture women often make less than men, and hit a "glass ceiling" stopping them from being allowed to lead in the bourgeoisie. Socialism should offer more opportunities for women to lead, with equal pay for equal work, and allowing ability to be the sole factor in whether or not someone leads…

Chapter 9

Art and Revolution

"In the world today all culture, all literature and art belong to definite classes and are geared to definite political lines. There is in fact no such thing as art for art's sake, art that stands above classes, art that is detached from or independent of politics. Proletarian literature and art are part of the whole proletarian revolutionary cause; they are, as Lenin said, cogs and wheels in the whole revolutionary machine.

-"Talks at the Yenan Forum on Literature and Art" (May 1942), Selected Works, Vol. III, p. 86.*

Clearly this is the case, the class structure determines the art in society. If one has ever tried to get a gig in America and is a socialist, one would see the dominance of the bourgeoisie in the artistic world.

Revolutionary artists in bourgeois society must give up ever being paid for their art, or being recognized internationally. This is entirely caused by class. Class entirely determines who will be educated in the arts, as school is too costly for the labourer. The popular musician on the radio will always be loyal to the bourgeoisie, it will never be otherwise.

In so far as the development of the productive forces and music, the type of music heard is intimately connected to the level of development. The electric guitar, for instance, revolutionized the instrument and the music we hear. It's everywhere, and it is the basis of new forms of music such as Jazz guitar.

Without the electric addition to the guitar, hitting single notes with horns accompanying becomes very difficult. The acoustic instrument is not loud enough, the addition of electricity has revolutionized this…

"Revolutionary culture is a powerful revolutionary weapon for the broad masses of the people. It prepares the ground ideologically before the revolution comes and is an important, indeed essential, fighting front in the general revolutionary front during the revolution.

-"On New Democracy" (January 1940), Selected Works, Vol. II, p. 382.

The ability of the proletariat to communicate musically is an essential part of the revolution. The knowledge of musical theory allows for the unrestricted mastery of jazz, and classical.

It is inevitable more knowledgeable musicians playing more sophisticated music such as jazz, which utilizes modal arrangements, would be revolutionary. The level of industrial development of the instrument, i.e. frets, place the player into a heavy industrial experience.

The broad masses of the people may not always recognize the revolutionary sounds as entirely favorable. This is no reason for the proletariat to stop playing it; indeed, he must preserve and continue to attempt to revolutionize the world of jazz. It is only through the continued efforts of the proletarian musician music will advance; the vanguard of the proletariat is jazz…

"Our literary and art workers must accomplish this task and shift their stand; they must gradually move their feet over to the side of the workers, peasants and soldiers, to the side of the proletariat, through the process of going into their very midst and into the thick of practical struggles and through the process of studying Marxism and society. Only in this way can we have a literature and art that are truly for the workers, peasants and soldiers, a truly proletarian literature and art.

-"Talks at the Yenan Forum on Literature and Art" (May 1942), Selected Works, Vol. III, p. 84.*

Art as a social movement must be directed at the labourers, it is the most advanced arts that are most technologically advanced, and through this advancement must come a proletarian artist culture.

The bourgeois may suggest their dominance over the world of art, indeed, the appreciation of, for instance, jazz is connected with the degree of literacy, especially musical theory. In this respect the artist is caught in a tough position, is he to attempt to play for the literate bourgeois, as he is knowledgeable though his culture to appreciate the more advanced forms of art .

Recognition of the artist on a mass scale is in the hands of the bourgeois. The artist is at their mercy. But this does not mean the revolutionary art is totally hostage to the dominant trend and commercialization of culture, rather it means his contribution will be more gradual, improvisation, for instance, slowly penetrating popular culture. It is through the popular culture the revolutionary art will eventually become understandable to the masses, and this will come through attempts to raise the literacy of the people, a programme of all socialist revolution.

Chapter 10

Conclusion

"Now, there are two different attitudes towards learning from others. One is the dogmatic attitude of transplanting everything, whether or not it is suited to our conditions. This is no good. The other attitude is to use our heads and learn those things that suit our conditions, that is, to absorb whatever experience is useful to us. That is the attitude we should adopt.

-On the Correct Handling of Contradictions among the People (February 27, 1957), 1st pocket ed., p. 75.

The national conditions of a society are what must dictate what we attempt to reach the people with, politically and artistically. The level of development of the productive forces, whether they are still maintained through constant attempts to increase the amount of relative surplus value produced, or have been nationalized, must be part of the criterion of political decisions towards a culture.

Ecological development, the saving of forests, replanting trees.etc. is increasingly becoming a political stand; the saving of a forest connected to the degree of industrial development of a culture.

In the developing world a forest is only seen as a source of creating wealth. This must be taken into account when dealing with a society.

This is part of the national conditions of a society, and is related to the level of literacy, and development of the productive forces.

One is not going to be able to transplant the ideas of industrially developed America and Europe on all the world. The degree of development of the natural sciences affects the social sciences, and must be taken into account in attempting to advance a developing country such as China.

Nevertheless China is remarkable in that the level of industrial development, albeit at the expense of ecology (until of late to some degree), has advanced so swiftly with socialism. Now it is the time to advance the relationship of the proletariat to the land itself, to revolutionize the ecology, though the planting of forests, etc.

"In order to have a real grasp of Marxism, one must learn it not only from books, but mainly through class struggle, through practical work and close contact with the masses of workers and peasants. When in addition to reading some Marxist books our intellectuals have gained some understanding through close contact with the masses of workers and peasants and through their own practical work, we will all be speaking the same language, not only the common language of patriotism and the common language of the socialist system, but probably even the common language of the communist world outlook. If that happens, all of us will certainly work much better.

-Speech at the Chinese Communist Party's National Conference on Propaganda Work (March 12, 1957), 1st pocket ed., p. 12

The experience of real contact with the proletariat, of having wandered deserts, been in revolution, experienced the brutal struggle of body on body between the classes, is the real method in which the revolution creates ideas. Combined with the knowledge of Marx and Engles, the experiences in revolution become understandable, and often the past is discovered to have been due to other factors than dumb luck. This shapes the society, as all members of culture have things to share, and society is created by man for adaptation to ecology. One must never forget the latter, in all social theories, regardless of how far removed from ecology man seems to have become, he is still a product of the natural environment, a creature who has evolved on Earth. Our current political and economic activity is our relationship to the natural world, and it through our conscious efforts we determine whether or not the ecology will prosper.

Nicholas Jay Boyes